Digital Currencies of the World

A Traveler's Guide to Blockchain-Based Money

Table of Contents

Chapter 1. Introduction

Step into the uncharted universe of digital currencies with our special report, "Digital Currencies of the World: A Traveler's Guide to Blockchain-Based Money." Devoid of jargon and furnished with engaging insights, this report will be your compass as you navigate the dynamic landscape of digital money. Whether you're an intrepid traveler trying to understand the virtual currencies of the territories you're exploring, a curious observer seeking to comprehend the blockchain revolution, or an avid investor scouting for emerging financial trends, this is the guide for you. Shedding light on an array of digital currencies, we break down complex concepts into easy, digestible insights, ensuring that the world of blockchain-based currencies is no longer a voyage into the unknown, but a pathway to innovative discovery. Unmask the intricacies, grasp the opportunities, and forecast the future with our special report—not just reading in the traditional sense, but an expedition rendered illuminating and exciting!

Chapter 2. The Advent of Digital Currencies

In the recent years, the world has seen a massive upheaval in the financial sector with the advent of digital currencies. These innovative forms of money, riding on advanced cryptography and blockchain technology, have stirred the world economy and opened a pool of opportunities and challenges alike.

2.1. The Origin Story

The journey of digital currencies started with the introduction of Bitcoin in 2009 by an unknown entity known only by the pseudonym Satoshi Nakamoto. Satoshi published a whitepaper titled "Bitcoin: A Peer-to-Peer Electronic Cash System" that detailed the mechanics of a digital currency powered by a decentralized ledger - the blockchain.

The advent of Bitcoin offered a uniquely decentralised method of financial transaction, providing the freedom to send money across the world without the need for an intermediary, such as a bank or a financial institution. This idea of transferring ownership digitally without a centralized authority was so revolutionary, it ignited an era of digital currency innovation.

2.2. Understanding Cryptography

A crucial part of this revolution is cryptography, the art of writing codes. More than just an art, today cryptography is a branch of mathematics, an indispensable tool in securing digital communication against adversaries.

Satoshi Nakamoto implemented cryptographic principles to conceive Bitcoin. By utilizing principles like hashing and digital signatures,

Bitcoin became a secure platform where transactions and balances could be maintained without any central authority. This use of cryptography ensured privacy and security for Bitcoin users, inciting further interest in the digital currency space.

2.3. The Birth of Blockchain

Underlying digital currency operation is the concept of the blockchain, a revolutionary technology that offers a decentralized method of storing and transferring data. A blockchain, in essence, is an aggregate of blocks. Each block contains data, the hash of the block — a unique digital fingerprint, and the hash of the previous block, creating an interconnected chain.

When a new block is added to the blockchain, it is practically impossible to alter the contents of a block unless consensus is reached across all nodes in the system. Once appended, a block is permanent and tamper-proof. This attribute makes the blockchain a dependable and secure platform, making it an ideal backbone for the operation of digital currencies.

2.4. The Blooming of Altcoins

Post the success of Bitcoin, the first few years of the 2010s saw a proliferation of alternative blockchain projects, taking inspiration from the success of Bitcoin but making alterations and additions to its model to serve different use-cases. Commonly referred to as altcoins, these digital currencies expanded the realm of possibilities within the crypto-verse.

Among these projects was Ethereum, introduced by Vitalik Buterin in 2015. Ethereum served as a platform that allows developers to build and operate smart contracts and decentralized applications on its blockchain, using a specially designed scripting language. Alongside Ethereum, many other altcoins like Ripple's XRP, Litecoin, and

Cardano emerged, each with its unique proposition to offer the world.

2.5. The Rising Implications

Undeniably, digital currencies have presented a transformative influence across various sectors. For one, they offer financial services to people lacking access to traditional banking systems. They also provide a means for anonymous transactions, giving a new power to privacy-conscious users. However, these benefits come with the undeniable risk that such anonymity could also be exploited by illicit actors.

Moreover, digital currencies have opened up a new asset class for investment, with many cryptocurrencies offering exponential return potential. This has attracted many investors, both retail and institutional, to place their bets on the upward trajectory of cryptocurrencies.

In conclusion, the advent of digital currencies has triggered a disruptive wave in the financial and technological landscape. However, as with any innovation, it brings with it a blend of opportunities and challenges. As we continue on this journey exploring the uncharted universe of digital currencies, we must be vigilant, adaptive and well-informed.

Chapter 3. Demystifying Blockchain: The Engine Behind Digital Money

If we liken the digital currency world to a buzzing, futuristic city, blockchain can be seen as the intricate system of roads, infrastructures, and regulations that enable the city to function. This technology is the lifeblood that fuels, and indeed allows, for the continuing existence and evolution of digital currencies. Let's peel back the layers and faint mythology shrouding blockchain, and venture into the core of digital money.

3.1. A Basic Understanding

Blockchain is essentially a new method of recording information - powerful, robust, and predicated on the principles of decentralization, transparency, and immutability. Envision a ledger, constantly updating and viewable by anyone, spread across a sprawling network of computers (nodes) which well and truly belong to no one person or entity. That, in its most basic form, offers a glimpse into what a blockchain is.

3.2. Breaking Down the Chain

Each 'block' in a blockchain contains a number of transactions. For instance, in the case of Bitcoin - the first blockchain-based cryptocurrency, each block will list a number of transactions involving bitcoins. Combined with cryptography, this structure verifies and solidifies transaction data to create a robust and secure system. Here's a simple explanation:

1. A participating node initiates a transaction, akin to the start of a

relay race.

2. The requested transaction is broadcasted to the network of nodes, like a race announcement.

3. Each node then verifies the transaction – the race's judges ensuring the rules are upheld. Verification usually checks the status and validity using known algorithms.

4. Once thoroughly inspected and approved, the transaction combines with others to create a block – the relay baton is formed.

5. The newly created block is now added to the blockchain, racing ahead to join the ever-lengthening chain of blocks – hence, 'blockchain'.

3.3. Blockchain: The Decentralized Powerhouse

Traditionally, transactions are logged and verified by a single, central authority. Say, for instance, you're transferring money to another person's bank account, the bank acts as the central ledger, documenting the transaction and altering the account balances accordingly.

Blockchain changes the game. It offers a decentralized peer-to-peer model where authority and trust are distributed among the network's participants. This decentralization empowers individuals, reduces friction in transactions, and even has the potential to lead to fairer financial systems.

3.4. Cogs and Wheels: Understanding Hashing and Cryptography

An integral aspect underpinning blockchain's success is a function known as 'hashing.' When a block is generated, it's assigned a unique cryptographic code, or a 'hash.' This hash is derived from the data contained within the block and acts as a digital fingerprint, one that is unique and irreversible. Even the smallest change inside a block will alter the hash completely. The hashing process ensures that once the block is added to the blockchain, the data within cannot be tampered or manipulated.

The hash of each new block also contains the hash of the preceding block. This creates a chain of blocks, or 'blockchain', and this interlinking is what makes the blockchain tamperproof. If any data is altered, the hashes will not match, alerting the system to potential danger or fraud.

3.5. Smart Contracts: The Autonomous Executors

The empowerment and automation of processes within the blockchain have been significantly enhanced by the advent of 'smart contracts'. These self-executing contracts with the terms of the agreement directly coded into it allow credible transactions without the need for third parties. This has massive implications for any industry where contractual transactions are integral.

3.6. Future Implications and Closing Thoughts

Blockchain's design makes it ideal for recording various types of activities including financial transactions, supply chain movements, vote tallies, identity management, and product origination assurance. This opens up a world of possibilities, transforming not just the financial sector but law enforcement, healthcare, academia and more.

Understanding blockchain is an initiation into the pulse of the digital currency world. Like a city pulsating with life, the true measure of its brilliance lies in its seamless operation. Blockchain is not just a technology, but a revolution set to redefine the world as we know it - unraveling the complexities is the first step in joining this paradigm shift.

Blockchain's grand design and potential can be intimidating for the uninitiated, but like any comprehensive map of a complex city or system, once you understand the markings, symbols, and structures, navigating becomes less challenging. This detailed guide seeks to provide an on-ramp to understanding and appreciating the transformative potential blockchain represents. Take a dive into these unchartered waters, and swim in the vast ocean of possibilities that lie within the realm of digital currencies.

Chapter 4. Global Players in the Digital Currency Arena

The digital currency arena is a vibrant ecosystem bristling with innovation. The stage is global with various players from different parts of the world, each bringing unique elements and perspectives to this fast-paced arena. These global players aren't limited to countries alone, but include corporations, financial institutions, and technocrats.

4.1. The Pioneers: The United States and China

Considered among the frontrunners in the digital currency race, the United States and China have taken distinctive approaches. The United States, home of Bitcoin, has primarily let the private sector steer the digital currency caravan. Regulatory bodies such as the Securities and Exchange Commission (SEC) have taken a primarily hands-off approach, permitting innovation while promulgating regulations to curtail malpractice.

China, on the other hand, has wielded a more directed approach. The People's Bank of China (PBoC) is at the forefront of central bank digital currency (CBDC) experimentation with its Digital Yuan. The Digital Yuan aims to provide a state-controlled alternative to privately issued digital currencies, enhance financial inclusion, and establish a new instrument for state monetary policy.

4.2. The Innovators: Estonia and Switzerland

Estonia and Switzerland are pushing boundaries with their pro-digital currency policies. Estonia, already digitally advanced with initiatives like E-residency, is advocating the use and acceptance of cryptocurrencies. It has progressive laws in place fostering a welcoming environment for blockchain startups and enthusiasts.

Switzerland, particularly the canton of Zug—now referred to as "Crypto Valley"—has become a hub for digital currency activity. Zug demonstrates a forward-thinking approach, accepting tax payments in Bitcoin and fostering a climate conducive to digital currency experimentation.

4.3. Transnational Corporations as Digital Currency Titans

Big tech companies are emerging as key players in the digital currency world. Facebook—with its rebranded Diem project—aims to build a reliable, secure, and usable digital currency that fosters financial inclusion. While still facing regulatory hurdles, Diem's potential impact is substantial.

JP Morgan, an American multinational investment bank, launched the JPM Coin—a digital token that enables instant payment transfers. It signifies a significant shift in attitude within legacy financial institutions towards the adoption of digital currencies.

4.4. From Tech Visionaires to Cryptocurrency Advocates

Tech visionaries like Elon Musk have a significant influence on digital currencies. Musk's opinions and actions, from endorsing Bitcoin to accepting it for Tesla purchases, causes market fluctuations, demonstrating the significant role individuals can have in this arena.

Groups like the Cryptocurrency Advocacy Group push for friendly regulations, seeking to create an environment that fosters digital currency innovation. They influence policy-making processes and provide stakeholders with navigational support through the complex digital currency landscape.

4.5. Moving Towards a Blockchain-Powered Future

The digital currency landscape is rapidly innovating, encompassing myriad technologies like blockchain and smart contracts. Ethereum, with its programmable smart contracts, shows how digital currency is more than just money—it's a platform for decentralized applications (Dapps) bringing substantial disruptive potential.

Central banks worldwide are exploring CBDCs, seeing them as a path to upgrade existing monetary systems and counter the growing influence of private digital coins.

In conclusion, the global players in the digital currency arena are a mix of countries, corporations, and individuals that significantly shape its course. With new entrants influencing the sector every day, the digital currency field is bound to get more diverse and exciting—rendering profound implications for how we envision finance and commerce. Whether these changes bring a utopia of decentralized power or digitized chaos is yet to be seen, but the journey promises to be an exciting adventure into novel forms of value exchange.

Chapter 5. Bitcoin: The Trailblazer of Digital Cash

Digital currencies have become a significant financial phenomenon in the 21st century, and at the forefront of this revolution is Bitcoin, the first blockchain-based currency. Born out of the endeavors of an individual or a group operating under the pseudonym 'Satoshi Nakamoto,' Bitcoin has spurred a wave of innovation and interested numerous users, entrepreneurs, and investors.

5.1. Unmasking the Genesis

In October 2008, a white paper named "Bitcoin: A Peer-to-Peer Electronic Cash System" was published on a cryptography mailing list. Beyond representing a blueprint for a groundbreaking digital currency, this white paper indicated the creation of Bitcoin, a pioneering system that relied on a decentralized network rather than a central authority.

Bitcoin's philosophy resonated with the ethos of cypherpunks, a community that espouses the use of strong cryptography and privacy technologies for social and political progression. The aim was to empower individuals by instilling financial control and confidentiality, which centralized financial systems often failed to provide.

5.2. Understanding the Model

Bitcoin utilizes a complex combination of game theory, cryptography, computer science, and economic principles to create a decentralized system that performs transactions. The underlying technology, blockchain, serves as a public ledger of all transactions performed within the Bitcoin network.

Transactions are grouped into 'blocks,' approximately every 10 minutes, in a process known as mining. 'Miners' solve increasingly difficult mathematical algorithms, a process that requires significant computational power, the result of which is the verification of transactions and the addition of a new block to the chain.

In appreciation of their role in maintaining the network's integrity, miners are rewarded with newly minted Bitcoin (a process that also goes by the name of the 'Bitcoin reward halving'). Over time, this reward decreases, approximating the deflationary model that Nakamoto envisioned.

The Bitcoin protocol is designed to create 21 million bitcoins, a limit intended to create scarcity and theoretically promote value appreciation.

5.3. Adoption and Acceptance

Bitcoin's adoption has grown remarkably since its inception. Initially, it was received with skepticism. However, as understanding and acceptance of its underlying technology have increased, adoption levels have risen dramatically. It has found acceptance as a medium of exchange, a store of value and, due to its volatility, a risky yet rewarding investment opportunity.

Merchants are increasingly accepting Bitcoin as a payment method, propelled by payment gateway technologies that enable streamlined transactions. Recognizing Bitcoin's potential, prominent businesses like Microsoft, Overstock, and Tesla have integrated it into their payment systems.

Governments and regulatory frameworks have, however, struggled to keep pace with Bitcoin's rapid development. Whereas some countries have embraced Bitcoin, recognizing a legal status for it, others have imposed stringent restrictions, acknowledging the potential misuses linked to its semi-anonymous nature.

5.4. The Market and Volatility

Bitcoin's value is determined by supply and demand dynamics in the open market. It has, however, exhibited notable price volatility throughout its history. Factors contributing to this include market speculation, regulatory news, technological advancements, and macroeconomic trends.

Despite this volatility, Bitcoin has shown a general trend of astronomical appreciation over the years, with momentary lapses. Its total market capitalization has surpassed that of many traditional companies, indicating increased investor confidence and perceiving Bitcoin as an investable asset.

5.5. Challenges and the Future

Bitcoin's journey has not been without hurdles. It has been associated with illegal activities due to its semi-anonymous nature, inspiring concerns about misuse. Its scalability is also questioned; the Bitcoin network is programmed to handle a limited number of transactions per second, leading to delays during peak times.

Away from the criticisms, there are developments aimed at creating solutions to these issues, such as the Lightning Network for scalability and greater regulatory oversight to curb misuse.

While predicting the future of Bitcoin is challenging, its disruptive influence in the financial industry is undeniable. It has prompted discussions about financial autonomy, privacy, and decentralization, challenging traditional finance's status quo. Whether this disruption leads to a full-blown cryptocurrency revolution or results in a measured integration of blockchain technology into our financial systems remains to be seen.

As we forge ahead into this digital frontier, Bitcoin's journey exemplifies the success of digital currencies and proves that blockchain technology holds the potential for future financial frameworks. Bitcoin's saga serves as a seminal chapter in the unfolding tale of digital currencies—reflecting the possibilities they hold, the challenges they confront, and the promise they embody for a decentralized economic future.

Chapter 6. Ethereum and Smart Contracts: More than Just Money

Ethereum, since its advent in 2015, has revolutionized the way we conceive the deployment and operation of digital technologies, offering far more than just a medium of transaction.

This pioneering platform has broadened the scope of blockchain beyond being a system simply vested in providing a digital currency. Ethereum equips its users with the capability to draft, manage, and implement smart contracts - self-executing agreements having the terms of agreement directly written into the code.

6.1. Origin and Ideology of Ethereum

The idea of Ethereum first materialized in the mind of Vitalik Buterin in 2013, and was brought to life in 2015 with the collaborative efforts of Gavin Wood, Anthony Di Iorio, Charles Hoskinson, and others.

The successful launch of Bitcoin in 2009 had proved that blockchain technology could run secure, decentralized applications, albeit with a limited feature set. Buterin's vision was to create a robust blockchain ecosystem with more capabilities so that anyone in the world could write and run software without the fear of censorship or third-party interference.

Ethereum's flexible platform was designed to be universally accessible, neutral, and open-source, with the most significant distinctive feature - ability to program custom "smart contracts."

6.2. Understanding Smart Contracts

The concept of smart contracts isn't exclusive to Ethereum or the digital world for that matter. In essence, a smart contract is nothing more than a traditional agreement or deal, but digitalized and automated. It's a self-executing contract with the terms of agreement or conditions pre-set between the parties and directly written into the code.

The conditions baked into these contracts trigger a series of automated actions without the need for intermediaries, reducing the risk of manual error, deceit, or breach while delivering speed, accuracy, and security.

For instance, consider an online transaction between two strangers involving a product's purchase. In a traditional setting, they would require an escrow service or a mutual trust. In contrast, a simple Ether-based smart contract can hold the required sum in escrow within the contract itself, releasing it to the seller only when delivery confirmation is received.

6.3. Ethereum: Beyond Digital Currency

While Ethereum does have its native digital currency, Ether (ETH), its application as a platform goes much beyond just transactional currency. Ethereum's platform and its decentralized applications (dApps) offer solutions across multiple fields.

A key feature, Decentralized Finance (DeFi), shifts the traditional financial paradigms to create an open and permissionless financial system. DeFi applications built on Ethereum allow functions like lending and borrowing, offering financial services minus the middlemen.

Ethereum is also a significant player in the Non-Fungible Token (NFT) sector, where digital assets with unique characteristics are bought, sold, and traded. NFTs built on Ethereum's blockchain can prove the ownership and authenticity of these digital assets, ranging from art pieces to virtual real estate and beyond.

Moreover, Ethereum's smart contracts enable the creation and exchange of ERC-20 tokens - customized cryptocurrencies that can represent anything from voting rights in a decentralized organization to digital collectibles.

6.4. Ethereum's Future: Eth2 and Beyond

Ethereum, like any other technology, isn't perfect. It has raised concerns about scalability, speed, and energy consumption. However, the Ethereum community is working on Eth2 or Ethereum 2.0, which promises to address these issues.

Eth2 is set to introduce a more environmentally friendly and efficient consensus mechanism - Proof of Stake (PoS), which also eliminates the costly computation in the traditional Proof of Work (PoW) model.

Alongside this, Eth2 sees the introduction of shard chains, smaller chains that operate concurrently to enhance capacity and speed. If successful, Ethereum could process thousands of transactions per second - a significant leap from the current 15-30 transactions per second.

In conclusion, Ethereum is much more than just a digital currency. It leverages the power of blockchain to introduce us to a world full of limitless possibilities - from Smart contracts to NFTs and DeFi. As we continue to delve deeper into this fascinating realm, each new discovery promises fresh opportunities, exciting breakthroughs, and a future shaped by the decentralized and transparent ethos of blockchain technology.

Chapter 7. The Rise of Stablecoins: Bridging the Real and Virtual Economy

The paradox of early cryptocurrencies like Bitcoin was that while they proffered an alternative to fiat currencies, their extreme volatility rendered them unsuitable for many everyday transactions. It was very much like possessing a treasure chest but with its actual value oscillating wildly from one day to the next. What use was a currency if one couldn't rely on its value? To address this quandary, the cryptosphere witnessed the birth of stablecoins—digital currencies that are informed by a constant value, one that is pegged to a specific asset, usually a known fiat currency like the U.S. Dollar, Euro, or Gold. By interlinking the predictability and stability of traditional assets with the decentralization, security, and speed of cryptocurrencies, stablecoins have become a bedrock of the digital economy, promising a future where the realms of fiat and digital money truly and efficiently intersect.

7.1. The Mechanics Behind Stability

Stablecoins derive their moniker from the promise—exchange rate stability with respect to a specific asset. Such stability keeps the price of a stablecoin immune to the loopy volatility commonly associated with cryptocurrencies. But how does it work? In the simplest terms, stablecoins maintain a 1:1 peg with their underlying asset, anchoring their value to the stability of this asset. This 'pegging' is achieved primarily through three types of mechanisms: fiat-collateralized, crypto-collateralized, and non-collateralized.

Fiat-collateralized stablecoins, the most straightforward in design, are backed by an equivalent amount of fiat currency held in reserve. This 1:1 backing means that for every stablecoin issued, there is an equivalent amount of fiat currency in a bank. Tether (USDT) and TrueUSD (TUSD) are examples of this type.

Crypto-collateralized stablecoins, on the other hand, are backed by other cryptocurrencies. Since the backing is volatile, overcollateralization is employed to provide a buffer. These types of stablecoins require complex mechanisms to ensure price alignment. MakerDAO's DAI is an example of a crypto-collateralized stablecoin.

Lastly, non-collateralized stablecoins, also known as algorithmic stablecoins, are not backed by any reserve but use algorithms and smart contracts to control the supply of the token, similar to how central banks control the money supply. Examples include Ampleforth (AMPL) and Basis Cash.

Each of these methods possesses its own pros and cons, requiring a delicate balance between stability, decentralization, and scalability.

7.2. The Impact on the Cryptocurrency Landscape

For the crypto world, the introduction of stablecoins has come not as an upheaval but as a much-needed method of balance and stability. By mitigating the significant risk associated with highly volatile currencies, stablecoins offer the desirable attributes of digital currencies without their unpredictability. They provide the assurance that the value of one's assets won't suddenly plummet overnight, inspiring confidence in a larger demographic of consumers and investors.

Because stablecoins offer stability and can be used as a store of value, they play an important role in increasing liquidity levels in crypto exchanges. This, coupled with the speed and low-cost transactions unique to cryptocurrencies, allows for efficient and cost-effective transacting, opening up new possibilities in remittance, payments, and lending.

While Bitcoin and Ethereum continue to dominate the cryptosphere in terms of market capitalization and popularity, the rise of stablecoins has carved out a viable niche, tuning the perception of cryptocurrencies from merely investment assets or speculative tokens, to a truly transactable medium of exchange.

7.3. Breaking Barriers and Forging Connections

Besides their role in striking a balance between stability and efficiency, stablecoins offer an exciting prospect — the union of the physical and digital economies. With their ability for instant transfer, combined with the familiarity of a stable asset, stablecoins neatly bridge the gap between traditional finance and its decentralized cousin.

Once the domain of a primarily tech-savvy user base, stablecoins democratize the financial landscape, attracting traditional investors and everyday users into the cryptosphere by offering access to permissionless, yet stable value storage and transaction.

Furthermore, the cross-border nature of stablecoins poses a significant advantage. Not confined by geopolitical boundaries, these digital assets can support seamless global transactions, enabling quicker, cheaper, and accessible cross-border remittances. This could prove revolutionary to international trade and finance, presenting a unified global currency that isn't subject to the exchange rate fluctuations of traditional currencies.

7.4. Navigating the Regulation Tangle

While stablecoins offer unparalleled advantages, they are not without concerns. Regulatory uncertainties pose a significant hurdle. Given their inherent global reach, these digital coins can potentially impact sovereign monetary policy and financial stability.

Recognizing the increasing prominence of stablecoins, financial institutions and international bodies like the G7 and the Financial Stability Board have started to look into regulatory policy. Any set of global, uniform regulations, however, would need to accommodate a balance between enabling innovation and managing risks to monetary stability, integrity, and governance.

Stablecoins stand on the tightrope of innovation and regulation. Their ultimate success will depend on their ability to maintain stability and to navigate the complex world of regulatory measures that await their progress.

7.5. The Future of Stablecoins

As the boundaries between the physical and digital blur increasingly, the importance and relevance of stablecoins are only set to rise. With Facebook's Diem (formerly Libra) slated to launch, for instance, the popularization and adoption of stablecoins are anticipated to vault to new heights.

Many believe that the evolution and integration of stablecoins will foster the rise of Decentralized Finance (DeFi), an ecosystem wherein financial products are available on a public decentralized blockchain network rather than going through intermediary financial institutions. In this context, stablecoins have the potential to disrupt traditional finance, giving rise to a new, open financial system.

Yet, the trajectory of stablecoins would not be linear. They will face their own set of challenges, from regulatory and legal hurdles to issues of trust and adoption. However, these hurdles, viewed constructively, can guide and shape the stablecoin industry's evolution, ensuring this innovation's resilience and success.

In this rapidly evolving scenery, the rise of stablecoins marks a significant milestone in the expedition of the digital economy. Combining the benefits of cryptocurrencies with the familiarity of traditional finance, they are bridging the gap between two worlds. The journey, however, has just begun. As we pull back the curtain to the expansive vista of what lies ahead, we are sure to encounter more innovations, more challenges, and inevitably, a world where the digital and the real are indistinguishably woven together.

Chapter 8. Cryptocurrency vs Fiat Money: A Comparative Analysis

Since the advent of blockchain technology, the financial world has been revolutionized. Among its forerunners, cryptocurrency, a type of digital currency, has increasingly made a convincing case for a monetary system of the future. To understand its full potential and unique offerings, a comparative analysis with the traditional form of currency—fiat money—provides valuable insights.

8.1. Understanding Fiat Money

Fiat money is a type of currency issued by a government, and its value is not backed by a physical commodity such as gold or silver. The value of fiat money is derived from the trust and confidence people and businesses have in the stability of their issuing government. Examples of fiat money include the U.S. dollar, Euro, and British pound.

Fiat currencies have a centralized nature. They are governed by central banks of particular countries which have the authority to determine monetary policies, control money supply, and are able to intervene when necessary to stabilize their respective economies. This control can, however, potentially lead to problems such as hyperinflation if the central bank prints too much money.

8.2. The Emergence of Cryptocurrencies

Cryptocurrencies, on the other hand, are decentralized forms of digital money based on blockchain technology. They are not issued or regulated by any government or banking authority. Bitcoin, Ethereum, and Litecoin are a few well-known examples of cryptocurrencies.

Cryptocurrencies work on blockchain technology—a distributed ledger system that records all transaction data across a peer-to-peer network. This decentralized nature of cryptocurrencies allows for transparency, immutability, and security.

8.3. Key Differences Between Fiat Money and Cryptocurrencies

Below are some of the major differences and comparisons between fiat money and cryptocurrencies.

Table 1. Fiat Money vs. Cryptocurrencies

Parameter	Fiat Money	Cryptocurrencies
Nature	Centralized	Decentralized
Authority	Government/central banks	Blockchain technology
Supply	Unlimited, government-controlled	Limited (in most cases)
Security	Might be prone to physical theft	Secure, thanks to cryptography
Transaction Times	Instant to a few days	Typically faster, can be instantaneous
Anonymity	Transactions can be traced	Offers a degree of anonymity

8.4. The Pros and Cons of Cryptocurrencies

Understanding the advantages and limitations of cryptocurrencies provides context for their current and potential roles in global economics.

On the positive side, cryptocurrencies offer peer-to-peer transactions without the need for a third party like a bank. They may enable quicker and cheaper international money transfers, and represent a global, non-inflationary form of money that can offer financial services to those without access to traditional banks.

However, cryptocurrencies also have some limitations. Their prices can be extremely volatile, creating potential risks for investors. Additionally, the anonymity they can provide has been linked to illegal activities and money laundering. Regulating them poses a challenge due to their international, decentralized nature.

8.5. The Future: Can Cryptocurrencies Replace Fiat Money?

The question remains: can cryptocurrencies replace traditional fiat money? While some techno-optimists might see a future where Bitcoin or another digital currency will overthrow traditional fiat currency, most experts believe the transition—if it happens at all—will be slow and gradual, and that digital currencies will coexist with fiat currency for a considerable time.

Crucial features such as stability, acceptance, and security will play a determining role. As it stands now, although cryptocurrencies have gained significant global recognition, they remain far from attaining the status of being a universally accepted medium of exchange. Their high volatility, environmental impact, and scalability issues further complicate matters.

In conclusion, while cryptocurrencies offer a novel means for financial transactions with their unique features and capabilities and have ushered the world into a new era of financial technology, they are not without challenges. The coexistence of fiat money and cryptocurrencies presents opportunities for a transitional hybrid model where both forms can serve different purposes and economic contexts. The interplay between cryptocurrencies and fiat money is an evolving landscape, making it crucial to continue our exploration and comprehension of these financial systems.

Chapter 9. Navigating Cryptocurrency Exchanges: A Guide for Travelers

The world of cryptocurrency is akin to an expansive, intricate marketplace, where all sorts of digital assets change hands. At the heart of this marketplace are cryptocurrency exchanges. They serve as the platforms where buyers and sellers meet, connecting those who have certain types of digital currencies with those seeking to acquire them.

Cryptocurrency exchanges can be understood as the middlemen of the digital asset ecosystem. They're pivotal to conducting transactions in this arena, integrating an array of digital currencies and facilitating crypto trades worldwide. So let's embark on this deep dive into understanding them better.

9.1. How Cryptocurrency Exchanges Work

The first thing to understand is that cryptocurrency exchanges are not all built the same. Some are designed to facilitate direct trading between users, also known as peer-to-peer exchanges. On these platforms, users set their own exchange rates and agree on trades independently. This form of exchange is less centralized and gives users more flexibility in determining their own prices.

On the other hand, traditional exchanges operate similarly to stock exchanges, where the platform sets the market price. This is usually determined by supply and demand dynamics in the market.

Another fundamental type is the cryptocurrency brokers. They resemble foreign currency exchanges, selling cryptocurrencies at prices set by the broker, usually at the market price plus a small premium.

Whichever exchange type you choose to engage with, understanding the working mechanism is essential. Setting up an account, conducting the necessary security measures to protect it, understanding the trading interface, and how to place orders are all part of the learning process.

9.2. Choosing the Right Exchange

With hundreds of exchanges available globally, the choice can be quite overwhelming. A multitude of factors should be evaluated when doing so, such as security protocols, available trading pairs, regulatory standing, user-friendly interface, customer service, and transaction fees. It's important to do your own research and perhaps consider starting with exchanges that have established reputations.

9.3. Understanding Cryptocurrency Pairs

To execute trades on a crypto exchange, understanding trading pairs is crucial. A trading pair comprises two currencies - one that can be purchased and another that can be sold. For instance, in the trading pair ETH/USD, Ethereum can be bought using US dollars. Most exchanges offer a range of trading pairs, which can be between cryptocurrencies, or a cryptocurrency and a fiat currency.

The availability of trading pairs may influence your choice of exchanges - some may offer more crypto-to-crypto pairs, while others may offer more crypto-to-fiat pairs. Knowing what assets you want to trade and ensuring they are available on the chosen exchange is an important consideration.

9.4. Security Measures

Security should be a top priority when dealing with digital currencies. Two-factor authentication (2FA), cold storage, and encryption should be standard features. If possible, choose an exchange that also provides insurance coverage for digital assets.

Remember, maintaining your own security habits is also pivotal in protecting your assets. Regularly update your passwords, never share sensitive information and stay cautious of suspicious activity.

9.5. Understanding Fees

Transactions on cryptocurrency exchanges come with fees. These may include deposit fees, trading fees, and withdrawal fees. Each exchange sets its own fee structure. Understanding these fees will help you avoid any unforeseen surprises and optimize your trading experience.

9.6. Dealing with Volatility

The cryptocurrency market is notorious for its extreme price volatility. As a traveler on this journey, it is crucial to have a strategy to deal with this unpredictability. Setting stop-loss orders and leveraging only what you can afford to lose are a few tactics to manage the risks that come with crypto trading.

9.7. Navigating Regulatory Aspects

Finally, it's important to remember that the regulatory environment around cryptocurrencies varies around the globe. The legality of cryptocurrencies and exchanges differs between countries, so it's crucial to consider these legal aspects before conducting any transactions.

In conclusion, cryptocurrency exchanges are the cornerstone of the digital currency ecosystem. Understanding their operation, along with an acute awareness of the risks involved, can set you on a productive journey in the world of cryptocurrencies. With attentiveness and due diligence, exciting opportunities can unfold in this dynamic marketplace.

Chapter 10. Legal Aspects and Regulation of Digital Currencies Globally

Let's begin by observing that every technology has a social and legal implication. This extends to digital currencies that wield the potential to redefine conventional understandings of finance and economy. Developed on the revolutionary technology called blockchain, these currencies offer a decentralized, secure model of financial transactions. However, the ambiguity about their legal status, different levels of adaptations worldwide, and issues regarding regulations form a complex landscape that should be thoroughly examined and understood.

10.1. Legal Recognition And Status Around The Globe

One of the first and most important aspects to understand about digital currencies is their legal recognition and status in different countries worldwide. On a broad scale, countries can be classified into three categories based on their acceptance of these currencies. Some countries have completely accepted these currencies, some have decided to regulate them, while others have completely banned their use.

In the United States, the legal recognition of digital currencies varies from state to state, but overall, they are not considered legal tender. However, that does not mean that it is illegal to own such currencies; they are recognized as a form of property and hence are subject to federal property laws.

European countries typically tend to be more accepting, but they too vary significantly. Estonia has embraced digital currencies and is considered to be one of the global leaders in digital currency acceptance. On the other hand, in countries like Germany, they are recognized as "private money," which simply means that they can be used in private transactions.

In contrast, countries such as China and India have been reluctant to accept digital currencies. China has issued multiple bans on investment in and transactions involving digital currencies. However, recently, there has seen some softening of stance, with digital currencies being recognized as a type of virtual commodity.

10.2. Regulatory Approaches To Digital Currencies

A substantial aspect of the legal side of digital currency is regulation, which ranges from anti-money laundering (AML) laws to financial and market regulation, taxation, and even consumer rights protection.

Regulation of these currencies can take several forms. Some countries, such as Japan, have adopted a comprehensive regulation approach, with digital currency exchanges needing licenses from the Financial Services Agency. Here, digital currencies are treated similarly to regular money, subject to AML and tax laws.

In other countries, like the United Kingdom, the lack of clear regulatory definition surrounding digital currencies makes precise regulation difficult. While the Financial Conduct Authority has issued warnings about investment risk in digital currency, no clear-cut regulatory laws exist.

One of the key regulatory challenges of digital currencies is their inherent global character. No one country or governing body holds jurisdiction over the entire blockchain on which these currencies are built and exchanged. Thus, the enforcing of jurisdiction-specific regulations on an inherently borderless system poses significant regulatory difficulties.

10.3. Legal Risks and Considerations

Given the abstraction and novelty of the technology, digital currencies inherently carry a high level of legal risk. The main concerns include financial crime, such as fraud and money laundering, market abuse, consumer protection, contractual issues, litigation, and disclosure requirements, among others.

In many countries, digital currencies remain unregulated, and there is no legal recourse for users if they become victims of a scam or fraud. From a consumer protection perspective, this makes investing or using digital currencies a risky proposition.

There are also overarching legal considerations about the rights and responsibilities of users. For instance, in a transaction involving digital currencies, how are standard contractual concepts like offer, acceptance, and consideration to be determined?

10.4. The Future of Legal Aspects and Regulations of Digital Currencies

Legal aspects and regulations of digital currencies are continually evolving. As technology advances and adoption increases, countries are compelled to revisit traditional laws and develop fresh legislation that can adequately address these paradigm-shifting technologies.

The main challenge here lies in balancing effective regulation with innovation. Over-regulation can stifle the prospective potential of digital currencies. At the same time, without stringent enough regulations, the associated risks remain unmitigated and can lead to misuse and economic instability.

In summary, the legal and regulatory aspects of digital currencies are as dynamic as the technology underpinning them. The key for stakeholders and policy-makers lies in staying up-to-date with advancements, comprehending the challenges they pose, and forming adaptive, effective legislation and regulations that enhance both security and innovation.

Chapter 11. The Future of Digital Currencies: Opportunities and Challenges

In the ever-evolving world of digital currencies, future predictions may seem akin to speculating on smoke patterns in an unpredictable breeze; however, considering observed trends, expert projections, and dominant patterns, we can sketch relatively feasible expectations. This chapter delineates the exciting new horizons and potential challenges of the intriguing journey into the future of digital currencies.

11.1. The Rise of Cryptocurrencies as Mainstream Payment Instruments

As we embark further into the digital age, the acceptance of cryptocurrencies as mainstream payment instruments is expected to rise. The enabling power of blockchain technology is pushing more businesses, big tech companies, and governments toward embracing cryptocurrencies. While major corporations like Tesla and PayPal have already begun to accept digital currencies as a form of payment, it's anticipated that more businesses across industries and scales will follow suit.

However, it is critical to note that this transition will not occur overnight. Regulatory uncertainties, trust issues, and technological challenges could slow down the pace of adoption. Blockchain technology, a vital underlying gearwork for cryptocurrencies, also brings with it a steep learning curve for businesses and customers alike. Moreover, there's the need for a robust framework that ensures customer protection, fraud prevention, and security against cyber-attacks, among other concerns.

11.2. Regulatory Challenges

The regulatory approach to digital currencies varies widely globally. Some countries like Switzerland and Japan have been relatively welcoming, with both giving legal recognition to cryptocurrencies. In contrast, other jurisdictions, including China and India, have shown more apprehension and maintaining more restrictive policies.

The digital nature of cryptocurrencies, which transcends borders, calls for a unified global regulatory approach. However, accomplishing this requires extensive cooperation and coordination among nations—a feat easier said than done. Disparate economic situations, distinct political views, motives, and priorities contribute to the complexity of international crypto regulation.

Regulatory clarity will eventually shape the future of digital currencies. A well-defined regulatory roadmap can help address risks while allowing cryptocurrencies to thrive within understood boundaries. The challenge lies in reaching a delicate balance between encouraging innovation and avoiding potential loopholes that may be exploited for financial crimes, such as money laundering and terror financing.

11.3. The Emergence of Central Bank Digital Currencies (CBDCs)

Central Banks around the world are intensively researching the potential for issuing their own, sovereign digital currencies — Central Bank Digital Currencies (CBDCs). Primarily, CBDCs aim to digitize physical cash and bring benefits like faster transaction speeds, lesser operational costs, better security against counterfeiting, and more efficiency in monetary policy implementation.

Despite the inherent benefits, CBDCs also pose significant challenges. One primary concern revolves around privacy. To maintain public trust, central banks will need to ensure private transactions while being compliant with regulations.

Also, as CBDCs have the potential to replace commercial bank deposits, they could disrupt the financial system and spark bank runs during times of economic downturn. Therefore, the successful management of CBDCs requires a carefully designed framework that ensures financial stability while maximizing the innate benefits.

11.4. Dimensions of Security

In a digital currency environment, ensuring security is paramount. From users' wallets to the transaction protocols, every component requires robust safeguards.

While blockchain technology provides a degree of security, cryptocurrencies remain susceptible to cybercrime. Despite security measures, incidents of hacking, fraud, and technical failures continue to plague this arena. Additionally, the irreversible nature of transactions and the anonymity that some digital currencies offer could potentially enable criminal activities.

On the brighter side, innovations are continually reducing these risk factors. Features such as multi-signature (multisig) requirements, physical biometric identification, and hardware wallets are enhancing the security of digital currencies.

In the coming years, the creation and deployment of even more advanced security measures, systems, and protocols will be primordial in ensuring the safety of digital-currency users and markets.

11.5. The Future: A Fusion of Opportunities and Challenges

The future of digital currencies is a landscape painted with both opportunities and challenges—a fusion that is as fascinating as it is formidable. As digital currencies continue to evolve and innovate, the dynamic interplay between the impact of financial developments, global socioeconomic trends, technological advancements, and regulatory changes will determine the shape of the landscape.

While digital currencies hold the promise of creating a more inclusive financial system, fostering faster and more efficient payments, and facilitating cross-border transactions, significant challenges lie ahead. These include regulatory uncertainties, potential cybersecurity threats, and the need for sound technological infrastructures.

Rest assured, as we navigate the uncharted waters of this digital sea, with every wave we crest and every storm we weather, the understanding and management of digital currencies will undoubtedly improve, guiding us steadily towards a future where the full potential of cryptocurrencies can be realized.